Fruit Facts

Steve Taylor

Rosen
REAL
READERS

The Rosen Publishing Group, Inc.
New York

1

Fruit is the sweet, juicy part of a plant where the seeds are. There are many kinds of fruit.

Fruit grows in many places.
Apples grow on apple trees.

Pears grow on pear trees.

Bananas grow on banana trees.

Oranges grow on orange trees.

Not all fruit grows on trees.
Raspberries grow on bushes.

Strawberries grow on plants.

Farmers pick fruit and put it in big boxes. They put the boxes on a truck.

The truck takes the fruit to the store. You can buy fruit at the store.

Fruit is good for you. Fruit tastes good, too!

Words to Know

apples

bananas

bushes

oranges

pears

raspberries

seeds

strawberries